# The Church Not Made With Hands

Other poetry books by John Terpstra:

*Scrabbling for Repose* (The Split Reed Press, 1982)

*Forty Days and Forty Nights* (Netherlandic Press, 1987)

*Naked Trees* (Netherlandic Press, 1990)

*Captain Kintail* (Netherlandic Press, 1992)

# The Church Not Made With Hands

Poems by John Terpstra

*for Laurel*
*with best regards*
*John Terpstra*

Wolsak and Wynn . Toronto

Typeset in Palatino, printed in Canada by
The Coach House Printing Company, Toronto

Front cover art:  © Michael Allgoewer, "Votive Box"
Cover design:  Stan Bevington
Author's photograph:  Katie Terpstra

Some of these poems have appeared previously in *The Broadway, Lit, The Spectator,
Christian Courier, Image (Am), CVII, Poetry Canada Review, Quarry* and *The Fiddlehead.*

The author wishes to thank the Canada Council for the Arts and the Ontario Arts
Council Writer's Reserve Fund.

The publishers acknowledge the support of the Canada Council for the Arts for our
publishing program.  We also thank the Ontario Arts Council for its support.  Funding
from these two organizations enables us to publish our books.

Wolsak and Wynn Publishers Ltd.
Don Mills Post Office Box 316
Don Mills, Ontario, Canada, M3C 2S7

Canadian Cataloguing in Publication Data

Terpstra, John
   The church not made with hands

Poems.
ISBN 0-919897-56-8

I. Title.

PS8589.E75C48 1997      C811'.54      C97-931804-1
PR9199.T47C48 1997

"she is everywhere and no place ..."
—*Mike Scott*

*For my parents, Klaas and Ann Terpstra*

# CONTENTS

## I

## II

## III

## IV

## V

I

For unto us
          in Aklavik
is born a child, in
                    Attiwapiskat
     Gaspé
               Cornerbrook, Newfoundland.
And a son is given in
                    Wetaskiwin
                              Bella Coola
Flin Flon.
          And the future of the whole earth
is placed upon the shoulders of the daughter of
Tuktoyaktuk
               Tignish
                         Swan Lake.
And the place of their birth is called
                                   Vermilion
Temiskaming
                         Nain.
          Picture Butte


An angel of the lord appears in the night sky
over Rankin Inlet, over
                    Iqualuit, saying
This shall be the sign:  you will find the babe
wrapped in cast-off flannel, lying
on a bed of straw, in
                    Esther, Alberta
in a winter feeding stall
an open boxcar, outside
                    Kindersley, Saskatchewan.

And sure, several hours north
from Hogg's Hollow, just this side
                         Engelhart

you see a one, sleeping in its mother's arms
on the soft shoulder, where their car broke down.
And the dark highway shines
                              imperishable life
while helping them
                    beneath these northern lights
and driving on, through
                         Cochrane
                                    Kapuskasing
                 Hearst
past Nipigon, and on
                      to the little town of Emo
Rainy River Region,
                     and least among the little dots
that lie scattered as stars
                       and litter the map
of Northwest Ontario,
where they're expecting you,
                          as in so many other
of these least likely dots
                        this expectation
also is, in
             Miniota
                         Pickle Lake
                                    Ohswekan


         Glace Bay.


For unto us
For into all
             this night
is born a child, this night
                         bearing each
and the places of their birth,
                          and nativity is given
                          every name.

When we first came to this country
your father and I tried to see
each new place as a kind of Bethlehem,
and we were the young, royal couple,
living our own prophetic adventure,
same as you, same as any simple fool
who claims they've heard angels
choir the sky, or the still
small voice of kept
promises.
                    And it helped.  Heaven knows
the so-called houses where we landed
were often no more than sheds,
and in that first year-and-a-half
there were four, which meant I'd bring
just a bit *gezelligheid* into our home
when off we would go to the next.
Don't mistake it now; we wanted
to settle down, but the better work
was always elsewhere.  So after I'd altered
the curtains for the umpteenth time
and hung another hectare of paper,
I simply gave in, collapsed
to the thought we were not here
to stay, didn't know where
it would end, if so, or what
might happen next.
                    And funny to tell,
but this helped too.  It put me in a mind
where the unexpectedness of each day
was actually welcome, and that picture
perfect world I wanted us to build
so it could be like back home, faded.


Your father and I tried to see this,
each town, each place, each time we came

and went, and driving to a new unknown
we'd do a game:
                    for unto you
Aldershot, Ontario,
                    least among the towns
of Highway 2,
                    to you this day, from
the displaced House of Orange, shall come
an immigrant family of four ...


                              Is there
enough hay?


                    Ah, but how the past is swaddled,
once the future's now and bright.


That was a nice place we had
on the King Road, in Aldershot.
It was small, but snug, and well-kept.
Your sisters and I could work the orchard
with dad, and it was pleasant work,
the picking, and pleasant to be outside
for our first Indian summer. We were high,
and could see the lake, and you grow attached,
you do, surprising sometimes how soon.
So I *did* cry, there, when the truck was packed,
again, before we'd even had a Christmas;
and it was so cold, even with the four of us
in the cab, and the further we drove
the longer it took till the next town,
and we only knew to stay on Highway 2, east
they told us, but not how far, or how
we'd long to see a sign, for

Gananoque

Lansdowne

Escott

                    and no one ever tells
what turns our lives may take, or where
or when it's leading us, and
                         Jesus, I sighed,
he said it best, he knew
                         the birds of the air,
that they always have nests, and even
the foxes,
               but where, I wondered
as the star lights of St. Lawrence ships
slipped by
               can a poor dutch girl
lay down her head.


Mallorytown

Brockville.


                    There are days
where I feel this
               even still.


There are days ...


                    don't you?

I moved to Burlington in my sleep. I moved
upstairs, to Burlington, Master Bedroom,
down the long hallway from Hogtown. I moved,
and in my sleep it was a Sunday afternoon,
Open House. Strangers were drifting
room to room, nodding in twos
through doorways, and fondling the woodwork.
They moved across the wall to wall
as if all the earth were under their feet,
but I knew they would have to leave, I knew
that four o'clock would roll around
and they would amble back to the curb, turn,
and try to imagine bicycles on the lawn,
themselves coming and going up the drive.
They didn't know this was *my* dream.
And in my dream it was preordained

                                           all this

was mine.


                               I moved to Burlington in my sleep.
I don't even like Burlington. I don't like
the little picnic towns that clear their orchards,
their farms, make tableland of every undulation
then gorge themselves on housing.
I badmouth Burlington so strongly
my daughter now complains of headaches
when we're driving through.

                                 But in my sleep
the big garage doors opened
and I was taken in, surprised
that they would have me, they knew
who craved this entry
into the large and tasteful kingdom
of his personal indoors, his furnished soul.

I moved to Burlington in my sleep.
It grew late.  The rooms were empty,
the strangers gone; and I slept-
walked down the halls to the front door
and stood on the stoop of my dream
home, and saw
                              many other people
having the same dream as me.
We were *all* asleep!  We were
sleeping together, a quiet cul-de-sac
of landscaped infidelity.
                              Tractor paths
still sank their ruts
into our rolled ripe lawns, and I know
in my heart the lousy truth, I know
there isn't room enough for everyone,
and the further we drift apart
the bigger our houses have to be,
and it's no excuse, I know!  but I hoped
never to wake.  Our grasses matched
so perfectly, it was
a rapture
                    of green.  I was
transported
                    to Burlington ...


                                        What can I say?
Some are chosen, some
not.  They're left
standing, stopped
at the curb, observed
through upstairs
windows, wide-eyed
                    nowhere.

## II - THIS ORCHARD SOUND

An old orchard, located near a six-lane highway
in an area zoned for the light industry,
fitness clubs, insurance offices, restaurants
and parking lots that are slowly filling in:
it has been left untended for a number of years.
Somewhere in the tangle of those derelict trees, he hopes,
is the branching cross-shape he has contracted to provide
a local congregation.

1.

I come to the garden alone, garden
of fruit, fruit of the tree: apple, pear,
peach, plum, cherry. The March earth
is a mulch of last autumn, a half-frozen
mass of leaves and produce that's yet
attracting birds, if that's
what the birds are after—
there are so many! lifting off,
landing, chatting like crazy,
making this orchard sound
like a major event

Lent

and in a little while,
leaves: blossom time.

Do these
damned trees still believe
everything
is possible? the power of prayer,
that the same old story
bears repeating, adding to
the two-grand anno domini
of borrowed time
we already have?

What will! to will
one thing, no matter
what, and carry through,
continue, ask, ask ...

The trees sweat
their tears of sap,
as birds talk up
this stillness.

2.
Signatures had kissed the bottom line,
and we left the garden, the orchard
Dirk was raised on.
                    And he told me
how it was, that in grade five
he cried for the harvest
he could only watch, torn
from his natural roots, and planted
in those other, unkind rows
in a room.

                    But that was then,
and you wouldn't have recognized the place
yourself, much less lose that self
in the calculated tangle of limbs,
as Dirk had, and clipped and tended,
summers, after school.

                    "It doesn't pay
to feel," he said,

                    when we arrived
and saw his former landscape flattened,
the trees shoved over, their underlimbs
ripped free, horribly exposed,
                              the dozer
grumbling still, at the turned earth,
a yellow god,
              insatiable of sacrifice.


When the driver broke for coffee
I could've let him have it
on the jaw, or bit
his ear off, but

*put*
*that rock down,* talk
instead.
       "Friend," I said,
"do what you have come for—
then,
        kiss off."

3.
The witness of Blue Delicious.
Plums. Santa Rosa. Early Golden.
Burbank. Shiro. The evidence
of Bartlett. Bosc. Kiefer.
Anjou (Ann-joe, in anglo). And Clapps,
favoured among pears.

                  The testimony
of apples. Northern. Greening.
Snow. Melba. Ida the Red
Spys
        Mr. MacIntosh. And the Red,
and the Golden (are you
who they say you are?)
               Delicious!
Not of this world.


                I find
                      no fault
                in these trees.


As you wander through their rows,
as you stand, facing each,
do you hear how it speaks,

                do you see
the apple lean to the plum
and whisper, sweet,
           do you hear ...

*No,*

*of course not.*
             *Trees*
*don't talk.*


                              You say
             that I am
                         fruity.


             What's truth?

4.
sign says

FUTURE DEVELOPMENT

(hopeful sign)
with number to call
should you wish

LEASE

Office/Retail

space,
acres of

Square Feet

Coming Soon

building
                    BOOM


                    to blossom
where pear would,
had it
                    a future.

5.
bark stripped, branches
brittled, snap
to the wind's whip


wither of unchecked disease
worm


bare arms describe
the shape of pain


                                staggered
half-dead
             trees


the awful, gorgeous sight
innocence
                inviolate.

6.

And at the orchard's heart
the ear is hounded by inhuman sound


a six-lane highway bass, breathing out
its monotone continuo of HNHNHNHNAAAAAAAAAA


while at the nearer lights, cars kneel
and throb their mocking yukyukyukyukyukyuk


as from the rooftops, heating units,
air conditioners, snicker the ozone


and the glazed eyes of office buildings
coldly smirk
                    *what bright sun?*


while heaven, heaven declares

                              only birds,
and the brown grass sighs.

7.
Admission time.  And fee.
I come to this ancient,
ongoing episode
                    participant
not free.  Mercenary.


This the great commission,
work received (proposal written,
submitted to committee, approved—
money changes hands)


                         And now
to find within their branching
a shape
            to hang on,
having persuaded others
of the cross
                    all creation bears,
I come to this garden
with swede saw, knowing
dimly only
                what implies.

8.

But jeepers! I had no idea
how heavy the thing would be,
and once the unwanted limbs
were sawn away, the ground
was a thicket of antler-work,
and I had to drag the unwieldy weight
through twigs and suckers snapping back
at me, and then the long haul to the car
past row upon row of its kindred,
while my sides burned, like carpet burn,
but broke skin, from the way I held it,
and my little girl was along, her poor feet
negotiating a frozen moonscape,
and she says, "Cold, daddy,"
and hugs my leg, and tries
to keep hugging my leg
as we stumble on,
and I pep-talk
                    a warmer weather:
mid-summer, let's pretend, and how hot
we'd be, and imagine the door
in that building swinging open,
and someone is coming out with a tray
of lemonade, and the ice tinkles
against the sides of the glasses,
where ice is best
and doesn't make us slip—
                              damn!


But killing time does pass,
and the deed is done.


                    "Turn
the heat on, daddy." I do.
I am.
            And we're driving home.

9.
For whose sake
                 is it
that the great garden of the earth
is torn?
                 to give whom
                 glory, that whose name
be praised, and who be esteemed
over-all flora, above all
fauna?
                         Day to day
the sound echoes and oceans kneel,
the mountains are brought low,
hills and rivers bow, and the great
cathedrals of wood are hewn.
                                    Branch
calls to branch. Leaves
in their gaiety flutter, flatter
whom?
                 as the slow arch is made
and the tree tips, it leans, over
and down, and the thunder sounds,
it shouts to the birds, fly!
and to the small animals, flee for refuge!


Refuge.
             Is there yet some place
where even I may go,
                         whose name
now rings
in every ear?

10.
How I prepped it:

using screwdriver, pried
under skin, barked
finger, but forced
the silent tearing peel

uncovering whiteness
wet

and some worm


Cleaned, and naked, propped outside
for time to let the living water
locked within
                    surface
abandon the body, dry
like bone


and over days, slits
like skilled incisions start—
these cracks, to make you think
split lightning, but torture-
slow,
            so you can feel it happen.

11.
Rewind.  Return to scene:  garden grove.
See me in tree with saw, poised
to haw haw haw through limb.  Now scan
the daily news, focus-in
this clip:

> "Physicist says, if you saw into a tree
> neighbouring trees put out a pulse
> of electricity:  they communicate
> directly.  Note blip on strip-chart:
> this tree put out a tremendous cry
> of alarm ...
>                         These trees know
> within a few seconds what is happening."


And where the branch was
shoot from stem

            is white

                    O

            an eye to look into,
    communicate directly.


Its rings spin 'round the head,
the neck,

            a lace,
and what suspends.

12.
Home again.  Meaning,
two-and-a-half storey brick,
twenty-two foot lot,
backing onto alley;

within which

two kids
helpmate
kitchen table, chairs,
dinner chitchat, bath
storytime ...

"Tell me a story, daddy ...
what you did at work today."

What I did today
anno domini
bears repeating?

*Tell me!*

How now
to carry through,
continue, ask, ask ...

13.
Come, see the place.
                    Roll away
the parking lot.  Uncover earth
beneath the asphalt, and below its surface
find the dried tendrils of uprooted
Bartlett.  Bosc.  Kiefer.  Friends.
It isn't here.


                    And into whose hand
surrenders the spirit of the place?
For as often as not we eat the foreign fruit
and drink the foreign wine, eating and drinking
the awful irony, that a ripe grove grew
where the car now leaks water from its rad.


Notice how that greenish liquid drips, begins
to run?  Like its distant cousin,
the rain, whose pellets strike
the pavement, congregate, and stream
in a worthy manner, that's natural,
but falling through a sewer grate


as dry tendrils ache
                    under this new earth.

14.

I come to the garden alone.  Traffic
is murder.  And the grass is still wet,
soaking my shoes.  As the cars shoot by
on the road adjacent, I try hiding
my swede saw, but it's long, and painted orange.
I've already taken two sets of branches
from this relic of an orchard, and am back
for more; as many, in fact, as can be found,
before the dozer arrives.
                                        This,
as my part in the inevitable, and how
to remember an event yet to take place,
that always takes place, *this* place,
the only kind that is, *my* place, and makes it
over,
            as if to prove other gods
are working, winning
these same lands.


                              *What it pays to feel*, he said.


I come by a tree, recently mauled, mangled
by cut and tear, and the familiar bramble
of lopped branches, so fresh
it seems the buds might still unfold,
that what little life remains
is enough to blossom.

But after these

events, this past
six weeks, I burst

*Who hath wounded thee?*
*Tell me, that I may take my blade,*
*its sharp teeth ...*

And the riled stillness
breaks, for once, and from all around birds
unfurl their wings, come flying in,
gather and land on the crazy busted branches,
talking it up;
and for once
I actually begin to make out
what they say; they say
but Nay, sir,

Nay,
for these, and we
make belief;
are these, sir,

not
the wounds of love?

**III**

They licked the trees, those two;

at first their fingers were enough
to touch the bark made moist by sweetwater
and then their tongues, their disappointment
that the maples had stopped,
officially, evaporating
in the proof there was some left,

that their fingers ran and tasted,
the damp falls spreading down
from the holes in their treesides,
where the taps had been removed;
holes a finger could stop;

and brought it to their tongues.

And after, they walked so slowly
that we stopped, several times, to wait
until their colours blinked between
the trees again, dressed
so brightly we couldn't miss
the *Here I am* they didn't have to say

or the sweetwater running its course.

They were going somewhere, or not—
were returning to us with each soft step
the earth could barely tell
took place, luxuriating
in what they'd seen there, and touched,
and tasted:  all a dream

to which they slowly consented to wake.


I'll say that our hearts burned:

as if two creatures, naturally
shy, should appear openly, unaware
of how we'd been sent away;
and passing through their sugar bush
a second time, we turned
to wait, and saw them enter

recognize the place, and run,
run! (how their arms once encircled our legs)
lean to, with sure allegiance,
the trunk's dark wound, and embrace
all that their thirst might intimate,

to lap the sweet spillwater of Christ their Lord.

Yellow green, the willows are emerging first again
out from our colour-free past, whisper
how brown it's been, is yet.
                                   Across the street
the magnolia bush, wild candelabrum, has set
pink white tapers at its fingertips, waiting
for the day to ignite.
                                   Everyone waits,
to see what will happen next, asks why
the leave-taker lingers.


                                   As the long dying weeks
of this latest winter slowly stripped us
we ate less and less, slept through the mornings.
Pinned to these weeks as we are, and knowing
the seasons, we accept this drawn-out ending;
but neither natural history, nor past attendance, nor
scriptured almanac prepare us for the always abrupt
brutality, the late storm screaming ice and snow,
or that quieter violence that intersects earth
at spearing lily head.


                                   All colour is contained in white.
Why shouldn't we prefer to pull the cover tighter
that the late storm drops and the third day
liquifies, revealing the ground, its sample resurrection
of crocuses, like brightened memories,
                                             purple yellow wakings
from a death we should be glad of?

We live on the simple surface of things, have felt
the earth's floor not deflect, stamping our feet
to shed snow, no deep reverberation to trouble
our limbs, the core; till now—the ground cracks open
wider than a crocus head, and granted Spring
the earth has always had, our loves have quit
the places we had buried them. We see them walking,
and feel the earth that bears us reverberate
each step: the landscape's an event
more sea than not, that we
must learn to walk again
and trust

> what happens next.


> Reach your hand.

This past half-season has taken us
like water, beyond reason and belief. We live
where water empties itself, rolls stone, or rises
as a hill; and the air breathes in.

> Should it

surprise us you take leave to rise
again, intangible as vapour, caught up
as the cloud we're staring after, then witness
what we see: a hand, a rose, a fraying sleeve.
All colour is contained in shapes the wind will free,
that linger our delight and desolation—

> and ours

are now your only eyes, this
your hand that's reached, let go, and these
your only feet, returning toward our lives.

I walked to the end of Dundurn Street,
to the quiet hind of a busy road,
where the bus loops. I walked
to the foot of the escarpment and looked
up, way, way up, at all those stairs.
And though they are wooden stairs
that make a nice wooden sound, and though
they lean endearingly to one side or the other
in a manner steel could never comprehend,
there are still two hundred and forty-six of them,
and before I was even halfway to the top
my legs had begun to feel lead-filled,
and the next step seemed a millennium away,
which, after all, it *was*, in a way, since here
*I* was, scaling the rocky old face
of mother earth, climbing her limestone chin,
her sandstone, siltstone, shale, dolomite skin,
*terra mama*, and all those labour-intensive layers
of her make-up, so that when I reached the top
I had to sit and catch my breath, and there
down below, was our little city, lying
spread out on its beach of glacial rubble,
sunning itself on a completely other
geological time, and I thought, well,
here I am, three hundred and fifty million years
from home.
               God! but it's been a while
since the foundation of the earth.
ALL THAT TIME!
                         and no one to talk to.


     I was alone, sitting on the brow
of the Niagara Escarpment, and except
for the constant swell and surge of cars
coming up Beckett's Drive to Garth Street,
or going down, it might have been peaceful.
I tried to concentrate on Lake Iroquois,

or Algonquin, whichever prehistoric pond it was
that lapped and bashed against this wall, but
the sun had set, and stars were beginning
to tinkle in the sky like wind chimes,
and a million lights were coming to life,
car lights, street lights, porch lights,
bicycle lights, night lights, and people
in their dim homes were moving
room to room, switching lights,
so the whole lovely view
flickered, all the time,
like lively little tongues, like
the lively little tongues of lovers
in the flame of affection,
and I thought
this is like Pentecost, kind of.


How is it we can barely talk to each other anymore?


Three hundred and fifty million years is nothing.
We're at least that far apart, sitting across
the same room. Switch the light. Is it
just me? Or where on this hardened planet
is there a hope our mutually exclusive, accrued
believings of the truth will break down, soften,
and flow together in the heat of some unimaginable
quaternary change? Or do we grow old this way,
waiting till the common weather finally erodes
these bloody unforgiving rocks
into a willing roundness?
                                    There's nothing much
to say—and it gets so tiring, climbing
the endless staircase of our wooden
chit chat

            chit chit chat

chit ...

          If only the window would blow open once,
and the conversation catch, like fire, so that
we're both, we're all consumed, and the room
isn't big enough anymore, and we take
to the street, and talk and talk,
and the languages we've learned to cultivate
exhaust themselves, so we have to dig deeper
and break out other mother tongues,
and get a bit drunk, spilling words
we never said before, didn't know
we knew, and we couldn't tell how long
we'd gone till people stopped
on their way to work, wondering, "What the ...?"
but then they'd join in too—because
it was contagious, it changed the face
of the earth, and these three hundred
and fifty million years
were like ...

            over.


           But here,

today,

           the words we use,
they fly, they arc
and dive through air, land
where we don't look, won't dare.
I pick up another, palm it, a stone
chip off the top of this cliff,

                  thinking

I should bring it back home.
Put it on the table between us.
Show you. Show me.

               How hard it is.
How long it's taken to get here.

This was to have been about the old flames,
and what they've hurdled, how they've leapt,
and about the old, retired men who gather
at the indoor mall, and take their coats off
so they are free to spread their arms
and be expansive, expressive, like in Slovakia,
Estonia, or Hungary,
                                    because that is where
they come from, and because all over the world
people are still speaking in tongues
they take to other lands, like this one.
And I may have gone so far as to say
they are a kind of evangel, these old, retired
Eastern European men, who added
to their number there that day, me.


This happens down past Barton Street,
by Kenilworth, that they stroll up
to one another across the tile floor
and slap shoulders, stand around.
Theirs is the easy, growing animation
that's geared to draw laughter out.

                                    Look,
it's all good news: they speak, it seems,
solely to get that rise from their compatriots,
that explosive laugh; which is loud enough, God
knows, and less polite, it drowns the muzak out.


And I might have said, at this point, "My Spirit
is poured upon all flesh,"
                                    for these are the words
of the text I thought applied, prophesied, in part,
these men.

          Flanking them, on either side,
are the rows of cubicle shops, with their young
sour attendants.  Staff is sour because already
it is a slow day, and they are bored, and time
for them drips tick by tick upon their forehead
like the kind of torture you've only read about.
Add to which, they work for some megapolitan outfit
that considers them more than just a little lower
than the angels ...

                        but our old apostles
pay no mind, caught up as they are in the dip
and rise of their own arcane, gregarious exchange.


What does this mean, that we hear
a lively commerce only they can comprehend?


                       They move on.
Their lollygagging group disbands
and wanders in a drifting, ragged line
out to where the mall opens up and the ceiling vaults
high over a tropic of doughnuts, tacos and pizza.
They reconnoitre a table,
                    and some of the men
sit, while others stand, one foot on the bench,
elbow on their knee, smoking, buying only coffee,
and gazing through the skylights, or into the leaves
of the large *ficus benjamina*, as if entranced
by the incongruities, this daily foreign action
they share with a tree, the conversations
steeped in godlike silences.
                  A woman walks past,
her age the one they may have been
when the fighting began, around the time
they also may have met the one they married,

with whom they left home, who also survives
and stands not far from here, bent
over the sink, is up to her elbows
in the dishwater of old world manners,
consenting that these ancient breadwinners
dream dreams
                              if they still have the eye.


Husbands and wives, and a war
elsewhere, that is said to be over.
                                        I've heard
about their friends, the extended families,
whole towns that were undone, in ways
unspeakable, or too mundane, because
that was Europe.


But there are no enemies here, and nothing
is foreign, and everything is.


The boys and girls who tend the shops
are almost all grown up now. It happened
as we sat here. They've aged, at least,
perceptibly, in their dolled cages.
                                        And if this
were yet to be about the dancing flames
hurdling time and place, I'd wonder at
these sons and daughters, what their vision
says, for this is also in the text, and I would see
those stated, mighty works of God
explicable,
                    but also at the Centre Mall.

Our old friends will emigrate again, at noon,
to a hot meal.  And through the fire and smoke
of the steel-making plants nearby, they'll carry
with them, jingling in trouser pockets,
only as many minutes as the world is handing out
today.


And so I never wrote it.
For the confusion of tongues and cultures,
commerce, peoples in their generation,
round tables rooted to tile floors, cigarettes,
styrofoam, and pot-bound tropical trees
reaching for the skylights


bested my glossolalia, simple as wine.

I'm God, she says, trying it on for size,
then giggles, can hardly believe herself.
What's so funny? we call from the hillsides,
our armchairs that hover over her play.
But like the grand old dame behind the curtain
who's overheard the menfolk gossip she's pregnant,
she turns her face to us, as if to say,
Who, me? Did I laugh?


From one horizon to the other
the landscape's a litter of drums and barrels;
the wagon's tipped over, everything's pulled
from the shelves, and Barbie, poor doll,
is naked again, and missing both legs.
It's a cruel world, even for plastic,
but we've seen this scene, that torso,
too often to be moved.


Listen child, if you're God, fix it.
Mend these bodies, straighten out our living room.
And we'll sing songs to you, we'll praise you
to our friends. I'd love to tell
total strangers the story,
how good you are, how well it is
you behave ...


                    But shall I then, or ever,
love you more than me?
Come on, Sarah Kate, let's clean up.

And so I take my firstborn by the hand
and lead her up the mountain, step by step.
*Where are we going?* she asks, and I say,
We are going for a sleep—and this, for once,
agrees with her.  But I never tell
the whole story, or say that every evening
she is laid upon the bed prepared for her,
or that her trust in me might be misplaced;
that I am bigger, but angels stay my hand;
or that instead of her or me the bushes
and the pens are stocked with animals,
because, it seems, our kind must make death.
And I haven't told her now is the heyday
of gods and their playthings, who chuck
all holy routine, refuse prayer, see only beasts
in her and me: gods of commerce, gods
of self, gods of God, for whom
the only sweetest smell is ours, burning
with zeal, or else another flame.
And I could name names, I could point, here,
there; I could say, "railway cars at midnight",
*los desaparacidos.*  I could tell her
every day
                    we inhale
the ashes of the innocents;
their last, expired
breath—
                    that it's in the air.


But the story's too much, even
for me, and I'm bigger.
I lead her only through the prayers
I dare to speak, and hope she sleeps.

Coming here today, still thinking of Anastasia,
who died, too slowly, half-paralyzed, poor rat,
dragging herself across the cage.  A pet's
old age:  interminably brief.
                              Built a box,
white pine, at last:  long having wanted
to build one they might break out of, if life
rebreathed—or wait:  it would return with them
to earth:  same gift.
                        Wrapped it
down in the roots of the Flowering Plum.


Come, let us share our dead.
Animal.  Personal.


                              Walking here, by Aberdeen,
Longwood Road, those raw old barkless columns of pine
occur.  This one, then, stands for Anastasia,
thanks, who with the others, if you eyeball
down the street, is faithfully propping up
its sagging piece of sky.  That's so the roof
won't fall in, again, though it feels like it has,
at first—it always feels like it has.  But
they keep it up, the dead.  They lean
this way and that, twist in and out
of our line of vision, but they're still employed,
these poles, these uncarved totems,
who stand for them.
                        And them's many.
The war goes, but undeclared, not well.
Taking the short cut here the count's
already more than my recall:  a few

aunts, uncles rarely met, the grandparents
on her side, and mine.  Her father—
his heart attack, vacationing
in his homeland, overseas; and his sons,
her brothers, all three, who died too slowly
of their disease, which he by awful graciousness
had lived just long enough to see.
A person could learn to hate
these inborn muscular ironies, that push
and bully our simple intricate lives.
And she carries it yet, that part of her
that splintered when they broke away;
and one of the poles we go by
stands for her.  The one, perhaps,
you saw me lean against, remembering this,
inventing, pretending
something to say.


                        They age in the elements,
these poles, these posts, these trunks of pine
stripped of all their clothing.
They line the way, stand by
to haul our messages, communicate
the latest or the last reports, to bear
our sometime recognition, grief and memory,
our invitation over the same earth we travel
coming to this place,
                    to give them name,
                    to share
our deaths,
who go,
           who also stay.

# IV - STARSHOUT CAFÉ

\*   (rhythm)

Saw you today, downtown, at the corner, waiting
for the light. red green. red green. blood. leaf.
Saw you standing at the edge
where the sidewalk steps down to the road
And traffic had stopped, finally
it was their turn to wait
And you took your first step, and walked across
and your legs, both your legs, swung
And the buildings on both sides backed off
they shrank
They didn't feel half so smart anymore
or so tall.

> Where have we met before?
> Laugh.  Don't laugh.

And I could be sitting, up in the cab
feeling the idle of eighteen wheels
waiting for you to pass
And I could pull the cord
let the airhorn blow—
another bull beast in rut
right in the centre of town—
but that would bring the buildings back
wouldn't it?

> Where do I know you from?
> How long has it been?

And I can see it, I can see it now:
I'm getting on, must be seventy-five, and sitting
*there*, on the park bench, by that statue of the queen
And all these years later, she and her lion
haven't said a word
they still haven't talked
But you walk by and turn my head, again—
you still turn my head
And I put my lips together—
I can still do that, I can still
put my lips together—
another old pucker, right downtown
I can still try and tweet.

        Don't laugh. *Laugh.*


    I want to know your mind,
voluptuous turns of thought.
I want to know the mind of God

    he said, everything else is details.

\*    (blues)

I have a confession to make.

> *Tell me about it.*

What's to tell?
I've been too quiet lately.

> *We've both been quiet.*

I've been quiet as our street
at four a.m.—our street
is so quiet then.  I've been
suspended in the liquid streetlight
waiting to be able to say

> *Say*

but tired, I've been so tired,
I lay awake, and the shiver begins,
the current of the hand
that wraps the base of the spine,
and I've longed to climb the capital "l"
for Lap, and sleep
the capital Sleep

> *So much of what takes place between us*
> *goes unspoken*
> *Most of what happens is not seen*


blood.      leaf.


Saw you today, in traffic.

*

Last time up north, this fall, by the lakes,
we saw a car, cars, follow one after the other,
over the whole evening, as we sat on the dock,
in those big Adirondacks, the chairs that entice you
never to stand.
                    They were spaced apart,
the cars, that is, their eyes bright,
butt-ends aglow, as they rode the shallow incline
up the side of the hill across the bay,
and around the point,
                              in no hurry.
There was nothing else to hear
when they were there, combusting
internally, tires kissing back
the pebbled asphalt,
                              but the northern silence
followed them, and waited by the cliff,
patient as a small crack, grew
till they were really gone, then spread
and settled deep as stars
in water—
                    and this lake
of bays retains enough of mystery
it must have been sacred to someone, once,
I'm sure—it tries to take us in.
And this landscape understands us, doesn't it?
imagines, better than we.
                              But how long
shall we be driven by
this need to exist
                    apart from others?

\*

And you can tell by the way the sunlight sneaks past
             the bars of the porch rail
             that the day is escaping
And you can stop and wait
And you can see the shadows angle out, oblique and crazed
And you can tip back on two legs, you can tip your chair
             as far back as the wall allows
And you can stare up into the ancient tongue-and-groove
             invisibly toe-nailed into place
And you can be glad when they come from under the trees
             that they waited for you
And you can lead them, room by room
And you can say, This is where I live now
                   This is where I cannot leave
And you can see by the open window
         you can tell by the way the moonlight sneaks through
             the bars of the crib-rail
             that nothing   ever   escapes
And in the dark open air of the front verandah
You can begin to explain


             I have wanted to be able to tell you this
*Tell me*
             I have wanted to be able to say


And you can say, This is all that happened
And you can say, I am not who you think
And as the wind and rain start banging to get in

You can say, And these are all the stupid fucking stones
           I carry in my pockets, in my head
And you can use up every ounce of anger and sorrow
           of joy and shame
And you can say, Who *isn't* to blame?


                                       *Tell me*


I hate the life that is in me.
        Somewhere in me there is a little life,
        and someone comes and cups their hands together
        and blows and blows and briefly it glows


And you can say, I can't do this
           I can't do this, not alone.

*

If I could pull myself up by the roots of this century
and shake the dirt
If I could take me to another time
plant myself beside water
and call together all wild life
that no longer runs to hide


If I could say to the earth
oma, sister, and love her
          as my own misused body
and raise my arms to the sky
opa, brother


If I could learn to crawl again
and let the bright red scrape bleed
with the green knee stain of grass


If only I could know
my place
and learn to speak

\*   (starshout café)


So here we are again, this must be the place,
this must be ... what was it called again?
Did it have a name?


This is the wild, the open frontier.
This is as far as we've come.


It's as if we'd gone to the pantry to fetch an apple,
and with that first bite that punctured the skin,
*snap*, we understood, at last, how naked we've been.


I have walked beside you, with you.
I have hidden and revealed:
This is as far as I've come.


And here are the clothes you lent me.
This is the time you spent.


We'll wait now, till all the world goes silent.
See how the prayers ascend from the flame.


Who is the other?  There are two, at least,
struggling in the dirt, under the starshot night.

Here is a list of the ones you love.
Here is the list of your enemies.


Stand round by the fire.
Let us synchronize the beating of our ...
          foot to floor, fist to door.


And remember how it is we came here.
Recall the route.
Remember we came of our own volition,
on our own—Remember we wouldn't say no.


Take this—I would like you to have it.
You don't have to be afraid.


Take this—it will sustain you.
It is not in private that the pain lets out.


Remember, here, on this frontier,
at the furthest reach of what we know
we don't,
          but facing each to each,
and these four walls ...
                    here,
at the Starshout Café, we say:

Hey welcome, Whitey, you old sourpuss,
you tightass bigot, you old jinx you—
      Look up, Take heart,
      This won't hurt a bit, but

                *don't laugh.*

                Laugh.

And it's written in neon flashes,
it's plastered across the evening sky,
it's brought to you by:

the universe, a friendly place?

*

I have found it, he said.  I have found
history.  Look, here it is.  Let me show you


the small stones our fathers kept
        inside their pocket, or slipped under their tongue
        to draw on, during those long cross-country walks
        they walked, without ever breathing a word
        they so rarely breathed a word
        of where, of why they'd gone—
or the small stones our mothers left
        under the pillow, inside the cake
        clues to what they'd saved for generations
        but couldn't name
or these
the small stones, like crumbs, like seed
        that fell on the trail behind us—
I followed them.  Here they are:
semi-precious.  Feel how light.


And I had been wondering why the floor lately
was always scattered with seed, from whenever
I put my coat on; as if I couldn't keep the flower
down, from bursting,
                        but they were falling sown
from the pocket I put my hand into, for the birds,
down by the trails at the arboretum


Follow me.

In this part of the country, come winter,
we stand in an open spot, off the trail,
and show our open palm to the scrub, supplicate
the trees:
                    chickadee dee dee
                    chicka dee

          And wait. They'll come
for the seed.  Their wings flickering light
in the branches, alight on our hand
And in their slight talon's grip


forgiveness, he said

*

That vacation we took, when we went to the mountains
driving in and around their wide bases
where their scree skirts touched the water,
the young water, just freed from the snow—
that was the best


And we were shouting, with the windows open
how young the mountains were, they'd been young
for ages, and we wanted to sing but the wind
was too loud and the car so highly wound
from climbing, its small engine drowned us,
it was like being inside a waterfall,
and we couldn't hear the radio, we couldn't
hear him sing
                    "so quiet in here—so quiet"


And I had forgotten how cold it gets at night
in the mountains, that even our two bodies entwined
were no help, and it reminded me of the time,
tucked into our tent, when we had no other choice
but to cry and cry ...
                    ⌐     we were orphaned
under the sky—but the stars bent down
to listen, then, and the trees, too, turned ...
Ah, but this is all just sentiment, isn't it?

*No.* Yes.

this is only two people,
huddled

*No. It isn't.*

*This passion is the will
of something wanting to be born.*

Red.    Green.

*Laugh.*

You'll tell me, one day, won't you?
what it is that I owe you.

\*   (blues, removed)

Let's get up now, you and I, roll off
the coiled bedsprings, stand stark as newborns
by the open window, raise both arms
and say ...
                   What shall we say?
Let's say we were sick, but are in remission,
were flat on our backs, but are up again,
and we're still at that stage of dumb, simple thanks,
with no questions asked, where everything looks
handmade: the flowers, for instance, their pistils
and stamen, the compound curves of petal—
such rapt attention to detail,
and all that open sex—
or the craft of our own flesh,
and the ultimate patience involved
in all things made.


And we'll go down to the creek, to the riverbank,
but later ... I'd like to follow that path
that runs right by the water's edge, and feel
how we're drawn, think
who could conceive
                   this wash
of sensuality, that laps
between earth and sky, or goes over,
lets go the sweet free fall,
making thunder at the base, and sculpting rock
for days and days, even without
our supervision.

And we could be sitting on those sculpted rocks
in the spray, and maybe it would outlast
our generation, or maybe only the day,
and we could be trashing weeds and crushing
wasps, again, before long, but for now
all the promises we said
when there was too much time for sleep
and mostly pain, seem able to be kept—


our present animation
magnifies
           all creation.

V

It all started in the backyard, when dad
sat me on the other side of the picnic table
where he was typing letters into the evening air.
He took a clean sheet of paper and a ball-point pen,
like the kind we used at school for stink-bombs,
clicked it, and as I was thinking matches, smell,
he began to sketch the privacies of women.


oh the wild wind grows and the green grass blows


He went into detail, but the pen leaked,
leaving bubbles of blue, especially
where the lines met, and I never thought
a thing of it, or what he said, except
that for the next few days I had troubles
with my sisters, and this
was my official introduction
into the physical mysteries.
I was clueless as they come.


And at the far end of the schoolyard the guys talked
a new religion, and hard on the heels of his personal
testimony one of them says SCREW. In big letters.
The malevolent reverence in his voice! I knew
he called upon a power greater than us all, but all
I saw was in the basement, in a jar, nickel-plated
and bright, but grown now, huge and cold, suspended
in the twisted air above us.


oh! wild wind, and
grass, green

It was just my imagination, running away,
but this was the first in a series of events
that led to my becoming a carpenter,
where you take what is suspended in the air
of someone's head, and make it.
Though I never made that connection
between dad's drawing and the girlfriends
I had, every year, starting in grade one.


                                        oh wind
                        grass


So Wally finally clued me in:

she   let   him   feel   her   up

And my poor imagination drew nearer
toward the sun-bare ankles of the girl
whom I knew from school, standing in a field of corn;
to slowly slide a hand above her hem,
reaching close but not quite there
where the playground ends, each time
his words replayed inside my head—
*she let, she let*—while staring out
the front room window,
                        the blowing grass
still green under the sun
                        the wind growing
my hand
            against
                        the glass between.

This is one of those stories that if
you don't want to believe it
won't make any difference—
it's all made up anyway.
One way or another everything's made up,
some of it from nothing, some
from bits and pieces found, bought,
bartered, passed on,

                          like the cottage the grandfolks built
up on Blind Bay, when they had no roads up there,
and you had to go in by boat
                        chug   chug
that old gas-powered outboard they hung on to, long
past its prime, and they were still always up
and off, first thing
                  chug   chug
when the water is calm and flat
and you can make good time, good time
is also made
           chug
but don't lean too far over
or the load will shift ...


... and it was once upon that time ago, back
at the start, when grandma and grandpa first
cut water, made waves, were likely no older
than we are, now, that they woke one morning
with the early birds at their window, and the sun
spread out over their quilt, as if
it was very specifically shining their meadow
bedspread of wild flower and flannel, the summer
cotton prints, while the leaves and needles
were waiting for them, outside, and waving, especially

the birches, and the water was making hollow notes
under the dock, and banging the boats around ...

and it went on and on like that, adding up,
building, till something about having it all
happen together, at once, finally
set them off, and they started to laugh.
Like that. A child's inheritance. Like
they still do, laugh, even now, at their age.
And that's how mom and dad were born.


When it calmed down again to normal daytime,
grandma and grandpa got up, and dressed,
and called the whole lot of us for breakfast,
but mom and dad were already off by themselves,
playing over on the flat rocks, behind
the cedars, where we saw the snakes basking
last year,
                and they looked up at the sound of their names,
their two bright orbs of eyes and mouths alert,
but it must have been the start
of one funny day, or something they already
ate, because they laughed, no disrespect
on their part, but what's so funny is
even the wind picks it up, and comes flying,
out of nowhere, through the cedars,
and it's the kind of wind that if
you face into it you can't catch your breath,
it wants to fill you up, and pull you
out across the bay, as if
it's saying, *Come on, get moving, come aawwwwwnnn!*
and maybe all this time you thought
the wind came from behind, and pushed,
like I did, but it doesn't, and it took
these two and lifted them over the roof

and onto the screened porch we added
a few summers back.  For the bugs.


We were there already, waiting for them,
the whole extended bunch of us,
from as far back as a long arm
could reach into the tree, right up
to the big round belly of the future
budging against the edge of the table—
so it was quite the crowd, as per usual,
to which were added the usual and less so
assorted sampling of imports, outcasts,
lowlifes and deepees, and maybe it's only
because up on Blind Bay all the grands and great
grands, the great greats, the mamas and papas
past, present, widowed and unwed,
feel that they're in their element,
that the more *we* are, the more *time* is, *and* space,
that before the sunlight has a chance to glint
in their first cup of coffee, one of them's gone,
likely fishing, and while the rest of us
think swimming, skipping stones, they'll hook
into something, though it's often so small
there's no ripple, the conversation
chugs along, and you can almost hear
that old outboard, off in the background,
and feel the quiet tug, as the line's played out,
and looking up at their faces, you break
surface
                    chug    chug

                                        "Hey, small fry," they say,
"Smile"—and they reel you in
                                        chug
They hold you up for all to admire.

And you have to admit that at this point,
for most, it's a heartwarmer, a tearjerker,
something's passing on. Then one of them cracks,
"Nice catch, nice catch," and they're in stitches.
We all are.
                    The table is calm and flat.
And before you have time to think, "Hey,
whose story *is* this?"
                    the load shifts
and they've tossed you back.


                         Remember how
that works?
            every time


              and the earth spins cockeyed, again,
always has, it's tipped
to one side, it's like one of the grands
leaned too far over, laughing,
                         and the wind
joins in, the house rattles, there's whitecaps,
we flip the boat upside-down on the beach
and head indoors ...



                    There's always someone there
who's spent the day upholstered with a book—
historical fiction, biography—
or tending to the wounded, the meals,
who holds open the door so we'll make it,
as lightning ignites our field of vision
and we scramble hands-first up the path
as it arcs between us, it jump-starts
the major appliances, like the big old
white metal icebox of time, over
against the wall, with its round shoulders

shrugging off what isn't needed,
whatever won't keep till tomorrow,
when the earth in all its precious know-how

       hums to,

chugs, land over lake, back round again,
first thing,

   and re-invents the view.


   "Not bad," says grand,
whose gold-tipped fingers tinker with the play
in all that daylight,

    "Not bad, for a bunch of have-nots."


    \*  \*  \*


Like I said from the start, this
is one of those stories that if
it doesn't always follow you
don't have to believe it
could make all the difference—
everything's all made up, some
from nothing, or just enough
to get by, the bits and pieces
left lying about, behind,
or handed on,

    like the cottage
the grandfolks built out on Blind Bay,
that took them so long because that
was before any roads nosed through
the woods, and you had to swim,
hard, just to keep up

      chug

         chug

Autumn is heaven, unless of course it rains cold
and takes out the leaves too quickly, but even so,
there are days in Autumn you wouldn't barter
for a fortnight of Summer.
                              Summer can be hell,
with the furnace running full tilt, triple shift,
and the scenery's melting together, including you.
But each good day in Autumn is minted individually,
to be enjoyed unalloyed, and they increase in value
the closer you get to snow.
                              Poolside in August,
the sun catches every facet of your dive
and chlorine bleaches out all impurity,
so you can begin to believe what you've got
is deserved—
                    but Autumn is more persuasive,
handing out its mid-mornings, mid-afternoons and
early evenings unexpectedly, one at a time,
so you know not to think what's earned, but thanks.


Now, I know there are some for whom, understandably,
this is drivel: the shut-in, or -out,
those who recently found how ill they really are,
or old; those who didn't do it, but rot in cages
all the same, or those who did, with just cause:
all those, in short, upon whom gravity has the upper hand:
their days are one insupportable bulk. And me,
tripping lightly from this line to the next—
I don't enjoy having to temper my enthusiasm,

but it does sharpen the edge.

Autumn has an edge too.  There's always
that one last day, minted in November,
that is so keen and rich and new
you can't want for more, but
to spend it—then Winter cashes in.


So what a nice day!  That wonderful late autumnal
slant of light, thin spun clouds, a warm
chill to the air.  Right now you can hear
people crunching their way through the leaves.
They've taken their jackets off and tied the sleeves
around their waists, walking the trails
by Cootes Paradise, or in the valley,
and they've skipped work or school to do it,
just like the same people will again
in Spring, that other season in-between,
when the great mother engine
starts cranking up again.


The engine shut down a few weeks ago,
and now we're coasting.


Every minute counts.

And how did he
                        receive the gifts
the baby infant child,
or was he still a babe?
                        how many hours
old was he, or months, or more
when the three well-heeled gents
arrived on the scene,
                        and when at last
they presented him their rich *impractica*
those precious things they'd come so far
so long to give
                        how much could he
                        by then

                        perceive?
Was he alert to the movement of someone new,
could his eyes focus in,
                        did they light
                        on the gold,
did his little hands flail about
                        or grab,
and were the parcels wrapped,
was he of an age to handle the ribbon,
tear the paper,
                        and would he then,
                        do you think
babble his own
                        pentecostal thanks, or ignore
the gift, the giver, crying "more! more!"
And would his parents finally stand on his behalf,
tired, accepting,
                        taking all this, these,
the others, the servants, drifters,

who come to adore, all hours,

                              day in day out,

as in a mother's arms the child
now begins to wail,

                        and wails with a will,

as they all do, the newly-born, the two-year-old,
wailing for all the world as if to ask
already

                that the cup would pass.


When the Lord Christ, in human form,
when the Prince of Light

                        revealed himself

in this, or somelike manner, at last
to the gentiles,

                just how did they

on our behalf

        receive?


Did we three
from out east

                shy back at all

from infant noise, or smell,

                        the sight,

the animals, the undreamt-of setting, off
a sidestreet,

              or, after the gifts,

their visit done, did they adjust
their royal dress, prepare the saddles,
and to each other silently confirm the fact
this was, all told, what they had come to see,

and might have guessed, having read
the ancient texts?
                    Did they, in point
                    of fact,
                            believe,
and mount their camels,
                                and so proceed, happy
into the new year, and home?
                                  or did it dawn
only later, months along, when the steady
eastward leading led them only further
into nights of fitful, interrupted rest,
the ground too hard for sleep, bones
suddenly old, ears hearing that cry
again and again.
                      And if and when
did they perceive that they had met a one
to whom their very richest knowing owned,
in whom
                all gift finds home, to whom
all gifts return,
                  who is
from before the world,
his light-year come to earth
like a star's
                shining,
present in the swaddling dark.

END NOTES

The title *The Church Not Made With Hands* is taken from a song of the same name, written by Mike Scott and sung on a recording with the group, The Waterboys. The epigraph is a phrase from the same song.

Many of the poems in this book were written at the request of Bart Nameth, while he was the Music Director at St. Cuthbert's Presbyterian Church, in Hamilton, Ontario. The first time he asked me to write for a specific high day on the church calendar, I balked, but wrote. The challenge of that first poem, and of the ones that followed, was to make it appropriate to the one Sunday morning for which it was intended but also readable to those who had other things to do on Sunday mornings. For the opportunity I never knew I wanted, and for the pleasure of being one half of a duo—reading the poems aloud to his accompaniment on piano—I owe Bart a great debt of thanks. It is his description of a poet that stays with me: one who says the right words at the right time, in the right place.

The first three poems ("The Little Towns of Bethlehem", "No dwelling place", and "I moved to Burlington ...") were written for the Bethlehem Sunday in Advent. "The Little Towns of Bethlehem" borrows from William Kurelek's series of paintings collected in a book called *A Northern Nativity*, where he asks "if it happened there, why not here; if then, why not now?" He was recalling a childhood dream in which the nativity occurred in an igloo in the far north, and his paintings place the birth in humble settings from coast to coast. "No dwelling place" relates some of my parent's experiences upon immigrating to Canada in the 1950's, and borrows from another question Kurelek asked: "if it happened to them, why not us?" The poem is spoken in the voice of my mother. *Gezelligheid*: hominess.

"This orchard sound" takes place during the forty days of Lent that precede Good Friday, for which it was written. The sequence is based, roughly, on the Fourteen Stations of the Cross. Dirk Windhorst (poem #2), who was raised on the orchard his father worked in Winona, Ontario. The physicist (#11) is one Ed Wagner, of Oregon, who made an instrument that measured and recorded the electrical impulses in trees, which he called W-waves. The outburst in the final poem is paraphrased from Oscar Wilde's *The Selfish Giant*, as is what the birds say. The orchard grew on the south side of Harvester Road, just east of Guelph Line, in Burlington, Ontario. The cross-tree hangs at St. Cuthbert's.

"Low Easter, Rock Chapel" is for the Sunday following Easter, usually known as Low Sunday.
"Our loves quit the places we bury them, and ascend": Ascension Day.

"Flames of affection, tongues of flame" and "Explicable as the Centre Mall" were written for Pentecost. The wooden steps have since been replaced by steel, and were reconfigured, and there are now 329 of them.

"Uncarved totems": All Saint's Day.

"The big round belly of the future" is for Rick Hayes and Bunny Robson, neighbours on the street. It is also an attempt to write for Trinity Sunday, though the bounds of orthodoxy are probably being stretched to their limit here. I was thinking of a description of the Trinity I once read in the writing of Matthew Fox, but could never relocate. The description ran like this: God laughs and gives birth to the child, the child laughs and gives birth to the spirit, the spirit laughs and gives birth to creation.

"Present light": Epiphany.